VENOM

Miseanie Falconer

In the end, people move on from people.

DEDICATED TO THE LOVELIEST LOVER.

Softness has never been my strong suit.
Stillness almost never came.
Visiting home at the crack of dawn, was my whiskey.

Do not run from your bodily craves.
My dear, do not cling to the idea that, love must be
pure of lust.
If I was sure about one thing and nothing else,
I was sure of desire in endearment.
Yes.
The tears will come and they will fall on your skin like
an invasion on your wellness.
You will become sick
And,
you must dwell.
After sickness, comes health and stability.
By then, you have experienced passion.
You have died.
But remember please,
It is not perpetual, and we are never ending.

In skin, in spirit.

Hather.
(Egyptian Goddess of love + beauty + motherhood)
Montu

(Egyptian God of war)
Thank you.

VENOM

If you have felt

love

lust

loneliness

then this is for you

I became him
and, he became me
till we were no longer each other.

VENOM

the difference with she and I was,

my skin would have burnt under seasons

Infinity if we were eternal
and,
her one night.

But, he could not see her venom and I was not his
lens.

He once told me,

"you are the water hindering my bloom. For so long
you have kept me and as a wildflower, my freedom is
indispensable"

There and then I knew
repatriation was inevitable.

CONTENTS

VENOM

Cheers to Womanhood

joy in the going

She made me remember why I was afraid to see him
after two decades
sure he broke me,
in the same brew he wanted to meet
and as I knelt, face down
in tears,
with the loudest screams filled with aches
I recollect,

"The likelihood of him tearing me apart in the name
of love was of the highest decree"
but is it love when there is just self?

She made me remember
that he too, was a junkie on heroine
plagued by depression
and that the near idea of me again,
would perpetuate the darkness he had inside of him

Sure he was egotistical
but I was an altruistic woman
there was light in our difference
so love did come easy,
forgiveness was near

VENOM

But I could not go back
we,
could not go back.

god's token

It started the night of the cold wars
the confrontation between what you know and what
you can feel
and for a split second, your womantuiton calls and
you notice,

The breathing is different.
the air in your lungs, is different.
how you pace yourself, is different.

After all this time
I still feel you
in every corner of my body, where you kept still
as I sat on the park bench, with my body recollecting
sweet sin
to myself, I said
"remember with pleasure, his sacredness."
the universe whispered,
"he is a novel and a novel is he."
not gruesome chapters of depression and the
overcoming.
no.
"he is a song."
a stream of consciousness mixed with oxymoron and
imagery

VENOM

an euphemistic irony
Aunt Carol never spoke of men who wrote stories on
pages with one breath
or who fills the coffee lines with one line, "what's on
the menu?"
a man who burns your everything, down to ashes and
still finds ounces of flames in your powdery remains

You see,
wanting you is like a baby who yearns for candy every
second of the god given day
or like jumping through fire to rescue your lover from
a burning building

you get all these burns and all these scars
But you were worth each mark
all hail the elected king
love, if anything, saved him.

them

They will come for you
bare-faced,
naked as the very day they were born
with the devil's stench,
and when they do,
you must be prepared.

You must be strong-headed
because they will not be weak at heart
and,
you will love their aroma.

people and their ways

The world is filled with dreamers, the deranged
and the drunks
lost loves become distant places
distant places become hoarders of forgotten
memories
and I wonder,
why on earth do people become your favourite
memory, your favourite food and your favourite
place?
why do their smell resemble that of Gods?
why do their hands feel like a privilege on
  your skin?
why is it that when they get up, leave you,
leave themselves
and,
walk out of fire like the creators meant to burn
everything else but them
you feel it more and you remember?

We are all comets on the seeing
but meteoroids on the greeting
this type of knowing
we yearn for
we do any and everything to be a part of.

nonsense

That's the thing
when they outgrow you
and,
leave you behind
you are shattered,
and scattered like ashes in the river
after a farewell ceremony

They leave you, with all these memories
all this baggage
and then you remember

people do not deserve you.

They are either full of shit or half on love.
half on themselves

That's when you realize
people do not make sense.

They never have.

growth

Isn't it strange?
some of us have been wearing wounds from the day
we were conceived
given battles to fight
battles that instill fear and grief in our kingdom
forced to become women
forced to become men
forced to become something in the wake of the
misery

Some like myself, have been dying since the day I
began living
saying prayers in sacred places,
wishing myself better days
chanting a better story
reminding myself and the universe
that,
loneliness exists
reminding myself that we can find happiness in
ourselves
in our shells
so we never end up alone

say a prayer for the living
we all need a little magic.

the day we met

My

legs

are twitching

and,

my lips are trembling

This is

the

beginning

of longevity in sin.

the man who.

How do I tell a man that,
I've been dreaming of him
since the first day we spoke?
or that my favourite song was a result of his voice
performing a rendition?

how do I tell a man that,
I've felt his kisses in the lonely corners of my bed
and, at nights I see a figment of his silhouette at
my doorstep

how do I tell him that,
his being is every woman's dream
so please
allow me the luck of getting mine fulfilled?
how do I tell him that the light he possesses is
indefinite
and, that's what gave me sanity ?
to know he was able to give light for as long as he
lived
without growing weary
internally echoed in my ears

how do I say,
"You are slowly reaping havoc in my mind and,
there is no way I can make sense of it without your

help?"

how do I tell him he is the most superb form of
beautiful without scaring him away?
lord how do I say,
"Your aesthetic is severely excruciating" to a man
who was built from the ashes of wonder?

how in God's name do I tell this man he is the
ultimate delight to a woman and although he
might overwhelm me
that I want him still?
how do I?

romans

endless ecstasy is what I would call you

call us.

it's a spiritual thing
your body was my religion
the nesting ground for praise and worship on
weekdays.
not just on Saturdays.

this was my temple.

If the flesh desires what is contrary to the spirit
how did we join the two ?

"The secret is learning to walk by the spirit"
  they said.

yet, the flesh was my spirit

so we walked in hands on low places
and, teeth and lips in high places
how do you deny a man who made you feel
  euphoric?
who sat you on the throne and took you between
cosmos?

but as long as I served him
I could not know God,
I could not serve my creator the way I knew I
  should.

a godly woman in the face of the ungodly,
screaming god
screaming body.

kneeling to appeal for the war to come was undying
and we were mortals, who played with immortal fire

till eventually we became immortals.

beings of the flesh.

happiness in sorrow

I found music and jingle in bells
at the sound of you saying
"you are not the woman I fell in love with"
and,
"you have changed and that is enough to know I
do not want to be with you anymore"

I found shame in knowing
that
you were unknowing of the difference
between
the woman before you
the backbone during you
and the warrior at the end of you.
I took no pride in knowing there would be an
"after you"

but who could be fooled ?
your legs danced to the hostility that grew static

between us

till eventually,
we grew
wave less,
soundless
less of each other
and apart.

jezebel in ja

I found myself in cities,
in the night air outside strip clubs
In wine bottles
In steamers
even beside dumpsters
or motels on the final lap of my drunken one night
stands

On seventh avenue
and,
sometimes at the intersection on South

I know it's confusing
because as a woman,
I was 'not supposed to' be hooked on the
  insanity
I was 'not supposed to' be on the lips of the
  critics
or sit on the very tongue they used to bring
  shame

but like they said,
"She is a jezebel"
and I was a proud one at that
Jezebels had no end
I was reckless
I lived on highs and worshipped my lows
but chaos was all I could breathe
and now,
I have made my peace.

simplicity

As, as you have
was, as I was
be, who you want to be

we have been,
for centuries
becoming more and more in our element

in our beginnings,
straight to our endings
living
with animosity
replacing serenity.

apologies

I am sorry that after all these years,
your skin remains
that you are still shamefaced in the revelation of
being a philander
I am sorry the scent of you lingers continuously as
daytime
and this is your day in moments
as the upper hands of God caress you
somehow I knew I was thrilled
thrilled that I have become a 5 ft. 3 inches pole of
glory
but disappointed that
you became less than a believer
less than who you were destined to be.

a coward to the things that destroys anyone and
everyone
a toxin dangerous to health that somehow, as the
father of destruction, and I, the mother of creation
was ready for.
I was craving the very obliteration that would have
destroyed me

I am sorry that you were afraid of the coming and the beauty after the going that your joyfulness remained lifeless

this was how he loved
in fragments, with shame, in fear of being the divergent lover
I am sorry you could not love you, the way I loved you and how others would
if you had given them the chance to.

shame game

Love is
not
just
you
and
me
it is the things we could not see
and
the things we are too ashamed to feel.

note to man

You
deserve
a woman
with
courage
whose
skin
will
burn
for
you
beneath
the
orange sun.

note to woman

You
deserve
a man
not just any man
one with honor,
who is fire
and,
fearless of his armour
being shed beneath
the ground
under his feet.
and just as a snail who
is
nothing
without its shell
his nothingness
will
be a reminder of what
remains without you,
his
skin.

ignorance

He never had time for the things I needed
feeling lonely in the noise was the only sense I
accomplished in coming days

I found absence in his presence,
"nothing has changed, you are my whole world"
but what's a world when you are never present to
live in it?
to flourish on all the things that 'it' consisted of ?

Love in kindness
stillness in discomfort

I was more than the universe and all the people
combined
woman, is what I call it.
and he could not see it

I lived in diners

and camped out in bars

On Wednesdays, for seconds at a time
my body resembled bourbon bottles

I hardly remembered the days of the week
much like he never honoured the power in me.

a problem with self

Eventually you
get tired
of
trying to fill
a
bucket that
is
leaking from
the
inside

sinking sand

Too stuck on the idea that things will get better.

and maybe after all these years
I will understand the defects that came after you
   left
I will comprehend the extent of my brain damage
I will have knowledge of why my ankles became
swollen
and
why my heart sunk every time I saw you at JoJo's
on Sundays.

love and other drugs

I am near maddened by all the beauty nestling in
his vain
he was a heart man
but he believed in his mind
the two could never be aligned
they could never agree on the things he needed to
better his being

he was high on love on Thursdays
but Saturdays, made him sick
he was sick of the arguing,
the suffocation and the wining that nearly
destroyed us,
destroyed him,
destroyed me.

The feeling he gave me, was different
it reminded me of the love we grew up seeing on
the old sharp TV
those black and white films, that nobody ever
seemed to watch
even when the room is filled with people,
 it just played.
they professed their love to each other, though
they knew only the ears of one another was
attentive
and,

somehow, that was enough.

Lending an ear to your lover was enough
enough to give you air times infinity.

VENOM

we are

People are not who they once were

We are in a continued cycle
from the goons to lovers
to the shameful and the connivers.

The full of heart, becoming heartless
the heartless, becoming full of heart.

Love is, boring the bodies filled with hate
hate is, trapping and filling the bodies of lovers

We are,
watching the devil's intricate hellos, knocking on
the doors of cheerful people.

Stealing souls and reviving those who have lived a
lifetime times ten but refuse to have enough.

We are watching the selfless become selfish
and the selfish become selfless

Without finesse
without speech
honouring desire as it if was some tequila

We have now become a people who,
honors death
and disregard life

devil holdings

I am to blame
for,
the monsters dwelling
as a result of being spoilt at the hands of yours
  truly
For too long,
the devil has been making a home in my soul

Eventually I had to know death
to be born again
 as,
 a woman of love and doctrine

a woman with power
and one, who knew her power

Who knew,
she was nothing less than powerful.

the yellow pants

Dangle you conscious man
dangle in the eyes of woman
fierce
powerful
you are the example of radiance
the god of sunshine
I kneel at the sight of your everything
steal my innocence.

This is the war we anticipated
we have prepared,
and now, we battle.
grandfather warned me of men whose armour was
built on aesthetic
built on fragments of lust and honour

a senseless fool in the area of survival
a coward who seeks defeat.
the agony to lose my whole.
afraid to be "less of a woman"
a girl.
like a child, forced to be obedient to the adult.
I am yours.

balance

It is,
hard to birth a flame
when,
only one element is blazing
and,
the other calm as the wind.

reverence

The universe likes us
likes you, likes me
likes the fact that I have become a woman slaved
to desire
of no norms, no rules or petty codes
allowing men to know me
to drink from the well of divinity and prosperity
drink slowly.
you
are
one
step
closer
to creation
to,
the all powerful
tread lightly,
you
are
on
hallowed
ground.

miseanie, me , myself

On some days, I loved myself before any man
I worshipped the ground that my feet laid soles on
I recognized the beauty nestling inside my veins

I was queen on the days he could not be king
I was an alcoholic on the days I could not be
    sober
and a mess when my body was non-responsive
and I thought to myself,
The crown does not drink!
But somehow my subconscious knew we had to,
even if it was incognito

But here it is,
the truth,
You are a control man
and I am,
a self-governing woman.
I am just as powerful.
just as vital
belonging to my own regime

in love, we are royalty
I will lose no power to care for you
no scars to be your crown.

I wore glasses to hide from the critics
a shawl to cover my kingdom

it burned

the rays of our love, burned.
but what's a little passion without pain?
what's the sun, in the absence of rain?

insight

Finding someone who will use their internal stars
to connect and make sense of the ones lying
recklessly inside you is rare.

they will do it
and, you will wonder
why on earth would you do this for me?
why in the name of love shall you disrupt the
balance   inside you to equate the mayhem inside
me?
then it will make complete and utter sense
that, the insanity in me, resonates the   stability in
  you
and without you, there is no me
we, together, are a grand constellation
that only our eyes, are capable of beholding.

gift

Sensual nights approach habitually
my body fell gracefully at his knees
and just as I thought I was in control
he.
I.
wildfire.

Once again, I am at the altar of lust and
  dishonor
of desire and passion gnawing between my legs
within my insides.

My tongue itches,
my breast aches
My body yearns to be on top of yours
figments of you beneath me, splattered across my
  head
the kissing and the grabbing
the throbbing and the late night cuddling wrecks
  me

VENOM

And I need you to understand that we are
creatures of sex,
of love
and, of destruction

and if that is so, why do we not embrace the parts
that make us holy?
without the fear of being who we are in the eyes of
society...
that is, not overly sexual
but members of a new race,
overcoming pettiness.
so, wreck me
sexually destroy me
if this is how, we are meant to show love.

saving

I wanted to say
I should have done better
and I could have been better
I wanted to believe
the unveiling was designed and crafted on the belief
of truths
and savoury kisses
but they were not
and I could not say much more
Mother Earth would not allow me,
such tragedy.

the you in me

You are not for me and I must come to terms with
    that.
I often think the media and television screens got
it wrong when their heartbroken characters say,
"I love you so much, till it hurts"

Is that really what they mean to say?
or is it ,
"It hurts to love you and that is why I can no
longer."
you see, loving someone is not supposed to mean,
walking blindly in a dark alley filled with only
thorns
sunflowers aren't supposed to bow their heads as
they become marescent
instead, they should salute the sky because we
bring life and not loathe and emptiness

I've come to these terms, once again
and this time, it knows me by name
as I , got familiar.
and for the millionth time, in a desperate
    attempt...

Grandfather taught me the art of becoming and

the study of the knowing

I must become who I should be
and,
I must know that loving you was not what I was
meant to do
and if so,
that loving you was a lesson rather than a blessing

and when your lies became raindrops on the
windowpane
that's when I realized that,
loving you was, me not loving myself
and loving myself meant that I could not love you
because you did not love me

in a sad way, that was my revelation

my holy doctrine.

The sacred words that have been bestowed upon
my tongue
in the most savoury way
telling me to ,
move on
telling me to,
find happiness in my own strength
inside the hollow openings of own bones

let them nestle me up
so that when he comes and if he comes,
he cannot be less than powerful
and,
nothing but grateful

to have a woman who knows her worth, who
would guard her worth
even to the sacred tombs

Grandfather, I tell you, was my favorite.

awaiting home

I feel as if I have felt the love of my life
but never to meet

I've felt him in scents, in spirit and in tinglings
I've heard fatherhood praise this stranger as inside
the walls of my hallelujah awaits his everything
when will he debut?
when will he who craves soul and body, all at once,
never apart, reduce fear and know me?
grandfather always said,
"Nothing happens before the time, yet time, waits
on no man."

I cannot be too quick
too ready
I must wait
home will find me
home after all, is where we are meant to be.

reality

I want to say he was worth a lifetime
but lifetime
only ever gave limits to beings like us
who grew beyond the wild
beyond all defined as living things
as, limitless creatures

he was specific to me
I remembered every conversation
 every scent
the way he spoke with the highest of esteem on
the things he had confidence in.

The way he honored morality and kindness
he understood worth
to him, I was his saviour
to me, he was grace.

we were,
 the balance mankind struggled to find
with the promised love of esther and the king

protection followed us
God reigned among us
we were his people.

lust

Lust
is,
you
filling
my
body
with
poison
and,
me
craving
the infection
without,
 end.

endurance

I want to endure

to fall hopelessly
and fearlessly in and out of love
I want to feel passion
dripping from my papaya
split
to feel waves in my legs and in my knees

I want to experience weak
a coward at the hands of bodily fireworks.

I want to feel the hands of my lover caressing my
kingdom
with the constant reminder that I am royalty.

majesty.

to live through shortness of breath
and,
sweat

VENOM

what a fucking privilege it will be, to endlessly
endure all this beautiful

so long as my heart still beats and I can
  breathe.
this, I will feel.

madness

Madness exists.
in the back our throats.
gnawing on the edge of glory
waiting and watching
watching and waiting
picking at our jaw bones
showing many faces
many skins
"The cat woman and the spinning wheel", they
    chant.
peppery delight to kill the devil's spy.
they all look alike
with white teeth and red lips
or
dark chocolate skin and moustache rings
cracked bones
walking on eggshells
chaos in the prettiest form of sin.
a stained smell; pungent.

woman

"Taste a woman.
I guarantee you will never forget."
crafted from the ashes of majesty.
she is eminence.
with a hint of magic, her hips will make you
  feel kingly
with a dose of honey, you will know not the term
"unsweetened"
fortunate enough, I was blessed with the legs of a
warrior and I, have fought.

I, am everlasting.

my face will linger,
your lips will tingle from my absence
and,
your mind will become your personal hell filled
with inner ramblings of your coulds and shoulds

and then I said to myself,
"Perhaps one day, a woman like me,
slaved to nature, will understand why grandpa no
longer hummed while he cleansed his clarinet."
just like that,
he said, "She was the very air I breathe, the very F

to my major and B to my minor, the source of all tunes and I lost her. I should have cherished her more, love her, a little more"

the eyes of death

The love I held for you,
cannot be understood
we live to rise and we live to fall
I can build you no longer

as the bones in my legs
and in my back reform to reborn
from the millions of time I have crashed into your
everything
I am no longer something
a nothingness that you will remember
and I am still suffering and surviving and thriving
all at once
loving you was the type of madness I could not
explain
that burns your brain, heart, soul and voice.
The type that steals your innocence
you know? Innocence like two toddlers on a park
bench

sometimes a lover needs not to feel the hands of
another but to heal and be
recoup to see.

I was in two places all at once
a lover who lived for you and a lover who lived for
all things but you
the price of womanhood
the price of being the loveliest lover.
without shame.

scarred love

I knew a little about treating men like royalty
who were scared of the word loyalty

then came the roof leaks and the nose bleeds
and the sprouting of lies from planted seeds

Ideally, it was the surface touch, then the late night
love
Then, all my energy you took

you did not give
the only word you knew was quit

You see, men are like swords
shiny on the outside,
hurts when they meet your inside
the war between good and evil
raw and intoxicating,
but effortlessly suffocating.
This stage, you do not deny.

shift in motion

You are hard on the tongue
hard on the voice
hard on the heart
you walk in the room, with fire beneath your heels
with your body built on love
and your smile built on sunshine
And then I say to myself, "can it be that he is
oblivious to his beam?"
to all his glory and astonishment that raises the
heads of women
that jerks the womb and give tingly feelings of
sensuality, of wants and needs

Sunrise does not exist without you
moonlit nights adore you
as I, could never ignore you
the muse of a chosen few.

and at nights, when the city sleeps and the
innocents are still
you and I dally along the souls of one another
because we were obsessed with the harmony of
our tune.

coffee shops

Coffee shops were the reason I enjoyed bars
they were one and the same
so many victims
so many people sharing pain
drowning their bodies in bottles of liquor
and,
yelling about failed past loves
and the ones yet to come

somehow they all said," I know they will fail
    too."

there was one particular alcoholic I adored,
with his Hilfiger jeans and many packs of
    cigarettes
in an attempt to silence his episodes of
    screams
for seven dog-filled years, he sat in the same
    corner
watching souls dangle in and out
he even watched me
one particular Tuesday he said,
"Come here beautiful. I have a message for

you.
The Falcon sees. The Falcon makes do. The
Falcon lies within you."

I did not understand, and though my bones began
to curl to illustrate fear
I held it.

my mind was a gun, sending bullets to my heart
that I alone, had to endure
then I understood
with so little words,
he told me to never lose sight of the prize
I was made to chase my dreams
and only I,
could give birth to the things that made me see
the things
that,
made me feel.

magic man

If you
look
carefully
you
will
see
the magic
lying
carelessly
in
his bones.

oneness

You
and
I
were the beating heart
of
conjoined twins
that if
ever apart,

we might not survive.

to my dearest

Burn
for
the man
who
sets you on fire

give skin,
for love.

oregon

I have not tasted heaven in years,
hell was always on the menu
and,
I was a sucker for the abyss.

lust in love

Yesterday, we did not exist.
today, we are drunk on lust, on whiskey, on bodies
on sweet, sweet Mary Jane.

tomorrow, we will be drunk-in-love
that was you and I
two bastards who took life as a form of drugs
and then became lovers.

winter

Winter is coming.

It's been years since I've loved a man this much
and on some days, I miss you a little more
that to me, was the difference between the wanting
and the knowing
and though my body twinged in your   absence
I had to remember the honor of being branded by
this shade of love
my dishonesty mumbled,
 "I'm going to the brew"
but
I visited the bar again on Saturday
moscato was my favorite.
somehow my bones ached because I promised you
I would stop drinking
but you, you promised to stop burying yourself in
every woman you met.

my body felt cold,
my eyes were dull,
every shirt I wore, indent with your smell.

how could it be that you are a figment of me
when it's me you no longer see ?
it was hard loving a man who loved nobody but
himself
It was hard making love to
the figure of his silhouette

He was there, but I did not feel him.
I felt hollowed holes in the passing of his skin as
the wind
I felt alone in the wary abyss of his madness
yet, somehow I enjoyed the insanity
and the soft becoming that ended in him blooming
slowly

midnight runs, countless hours of collision on rugs
Broken bottles on the floor, it's 4 am
ready?
again.

another day

Today the encounter was different.
outer body
tough
I see them, practicing the art of pretence.
women falsifying soldiers
men becoming stone-faced Gods.
this is war
the Armageddon.

adoration

It was crazy
I was an admirer of all things
I could not find it within my being to put a woman
down
nor, publicly ridicule her for the things she did not
possess
instead, I found myself giving constant reminder
of her image being designed by the creator
I ranted for hours about her dust being gathered
under a frame crafted by the superior
I could only show her love
and say,
"Where you fall short in one area, you are supreme
in the other. Do not cry if they do not see it, they
are not meant to."
never forget,
you will one day find your beholder and he will see
the fire inside you
that you, yourself are too timid to see.

glance

I glance at you, in a way you do not glance at me
I see you, in a light you do not see me.

Whilst my soul yearns to meet yours,
I remember to always do right by me
to understand that I come from a brand of
universal love not appreciated enough by its own
species
I try to remember that this conservative society
runs vice versa
and often times,
we as humans,
run parallel to this indefinite stature we
wholesomely wish to embrace

I fear that I do not own the skin you would like
for me to bear
but, happy that I've come to know that this corium
is a clear representation of greatness and beauty

A trademark that distinguishes a warrior's skin
from the oppressor
the coat of arms of a country not appreciated
enough by its people

I spent a decade and six years running from a body

VENOM

I did not desire
I became a junkie on writing so the reality of this
madness did not destroy me.

But I want to tell myself this with so much truth, "
You are you, regardless of who sees you."
you are as beautiful regardless of your defects
there is the truth

No one is more human than you.

ending the revolt

I cannot keep up with you,
as the air in my lungs become shallow
and the bones in my jaw cringe to demonstrate
laughter
I feel,
heartbreak
discomfort
despair
figurines of disappointment becoming monuments
of latter glory

I feel the sun on my skin
but the rays do not burn me

painfully, your name does

the idea of you, stings
like a bee on the nose of a gazing man running in
the wild

the soles of my feet are sore
my back falls short of stance
I must slow down to let you run
this race was not meant for me

VENOM

it was not supposed to be

me.
loving
you.
eternally
and.
you.
loving.
me.
seasonally.

Wars were not won by one man.

space and race

Do not become filled with sorrow if you grow
distant from your body,
yourself,
people.

Space is not a human thing,
 it is spiritual
and sometimes to get in tune
we must become supernatural.

love triad

you had the eyes of another woman
looking back at you
while you were inside me

you made me melt
and at the very sound of my cummings
you heard her,
telling you
"I love you"
a million times
and somehow,
you found exoneration for your crimes

you loved her through me
because your sins would not set you free
and I was captive in a body
whose soul could not be released

a distant memory

and that was
an ache,
everywhere
altogether.

warnings

"I want you"

these were grave words.

too little in speech
too fiery on the heart.

I've had enough of me exposed to warn you that
not everyone will enjoy you bare
or appreciate the nakedness to come in love

so,
do not overthink these words
do not become loving of these words.

become loving of you
want you

say this to yourself.

beast

He was a painful man.

I think he enjoyed hurting me
and,
every time I cried, it gave him an erection

"Come on big girl. Show me those tears. Show me
how my living in you forever, has made you
weak."

I've felt so hollow in my sleep and in my dreams
and every kiss brought me to a city where the
passing was difficult to come by.
he touched me softly and made love to me in
footsteps so gentle, only a baby's creep could
mimic these rounds.
no wonder they giggled,
it was their language
he learned it
and,
he intoxicated my being
with,
 every drop of paradise.

scarlet woman

I gave up my body,
in cemeteries
on tombstones
celebrating life with crackheads and the dead

"They listened more than any living and sane person
ever did"
I said to myself
but even I, tend to feel like everyone else
on the days I did not feel like myself
and it threatened my peace
my mental health was at risk

I forgot that I was my body
and,
my body was me
each part could not speak for it self
as there is interdependence

There were many escape routes
I was,
conscious in the day, unconscious by night

VENOM

Being a masochist did nothing for me,
when the pain was more than the physical

this kind of unfeeling was the very reason for my
becoming
a scarlet woman
without regret
and
with awareness.

the aftermath

I lied to your mother when she called
she said, "my dear, it's been years. Are you well?"

but I was not doing well
things were not great

I was short on air in a room full of oxygen
and breathing still in a room full of poison

I closed my eyes and the image of your face runs
constant
and,
I remember that it will only be a memory
the shame that I will never live through us again
through you,
was tenderness

cigars became my crowning glory
scotch and gin was skin
till I was nothing more than
nothing.

CHEERS TO WOMANHOOD

I think above all things, I was happiest to be alive. I am grateful that this did not kill me the way it was supposed to and somehow, in its entirety, I found myself still breathing. I made it and sharing the journey is not easy but saying your peace with the universe can heal you tremendously. At nights I use to make vows, to not belong to anyone else and to place worth on myself. I had to remember that, I had value and that value made me invaluable. I felt like a body, me being the left and my mother being the right, she was the stronger side of me and with her, I could face anything, all things. At some point in life, whether adolescence, adulthood, the shift to fatherhood and motherhood, you will meet someone who will take your breath away and intoxicate you in ways you thought was humanly impossible. By then, you would have had to find another way to breathe in their absence because often times they do not come back and if you are lucky enough, you might see a glimpse of them in an old favorite club, by the coffee shop or at a gas station. That there, will be your oxygen, and it is okay to breathe from a distance. You will be okay. I know I have been, so you can too. Please overcome it, fight it and be better than it. Cry if you need to, pain is necessary and each of us on this earth, is vital. I'm still learning, still growing and still alive. Cheers to womanhood! You are stronger than you think.

The end.